Cute Cats

A Gray scale Coloring Book

For

Adults

By

Engy Khalil

Copyrighted Material

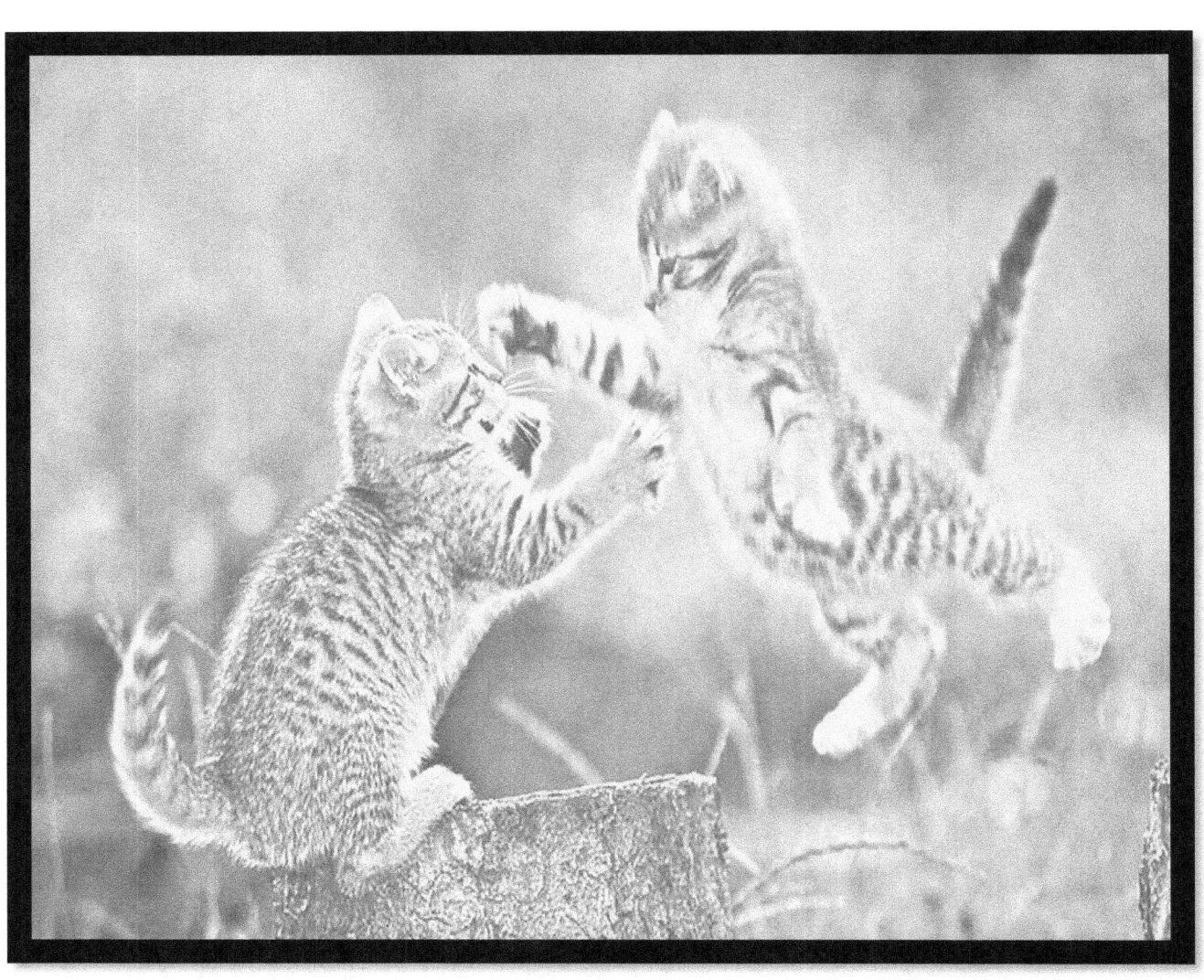

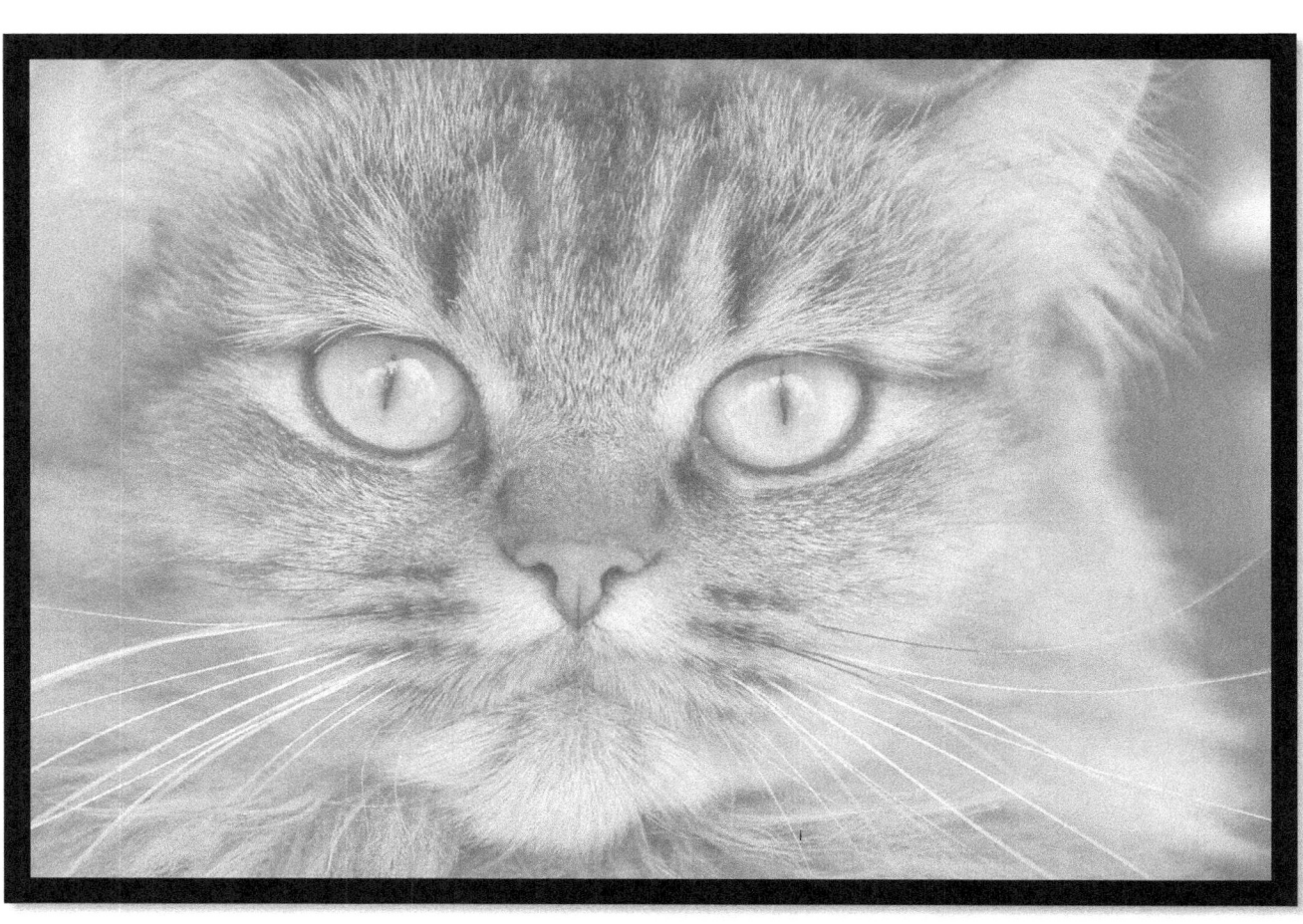

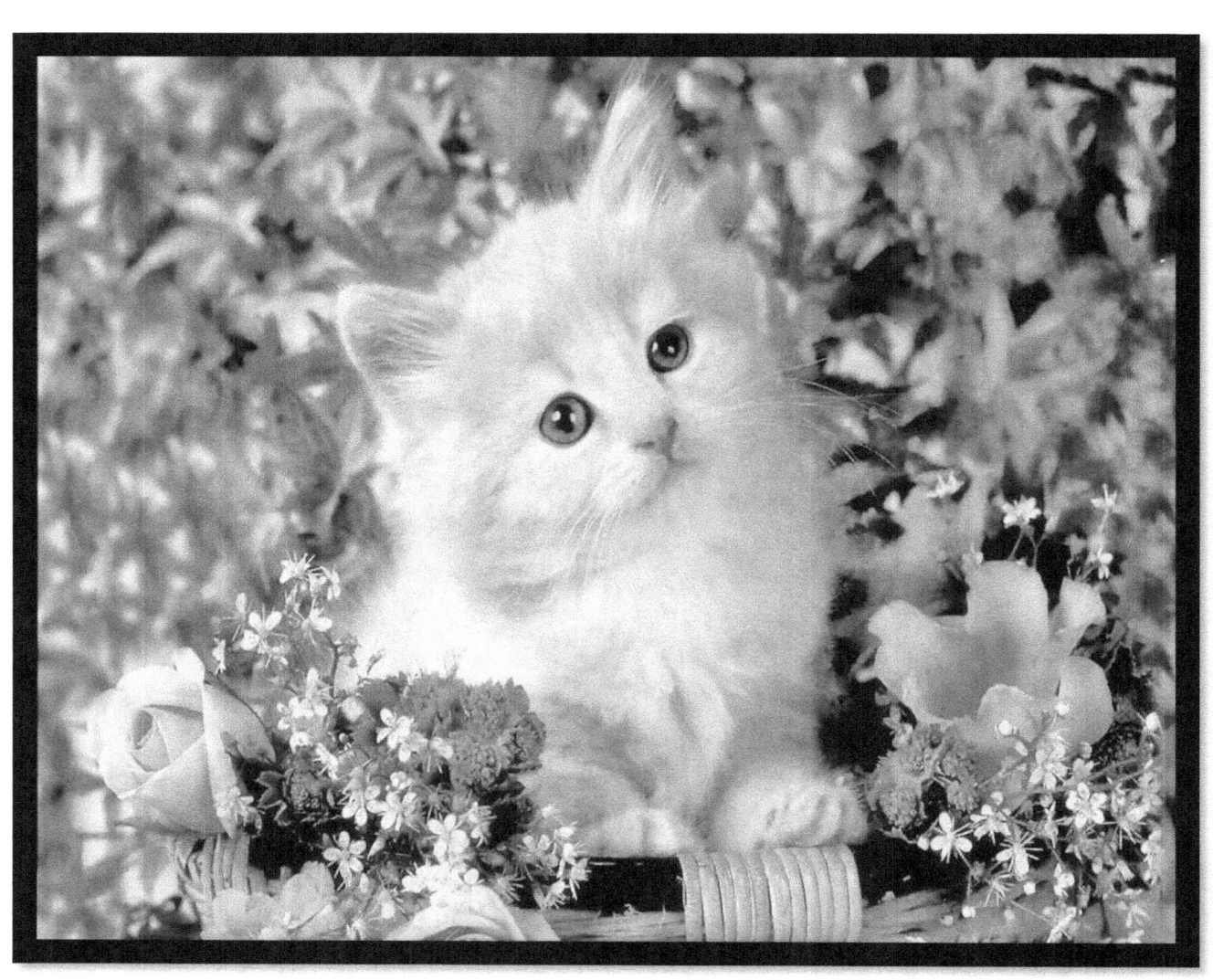

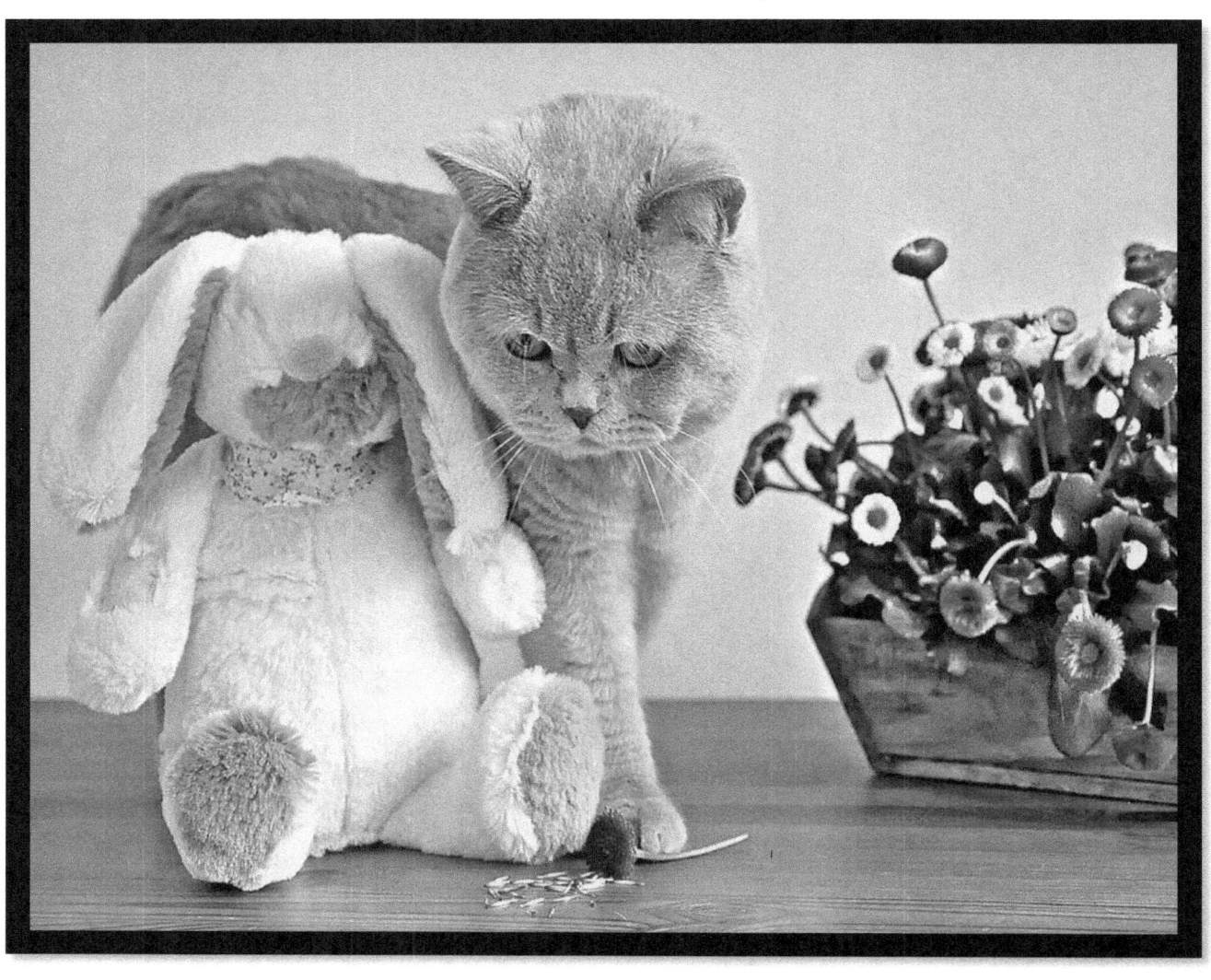

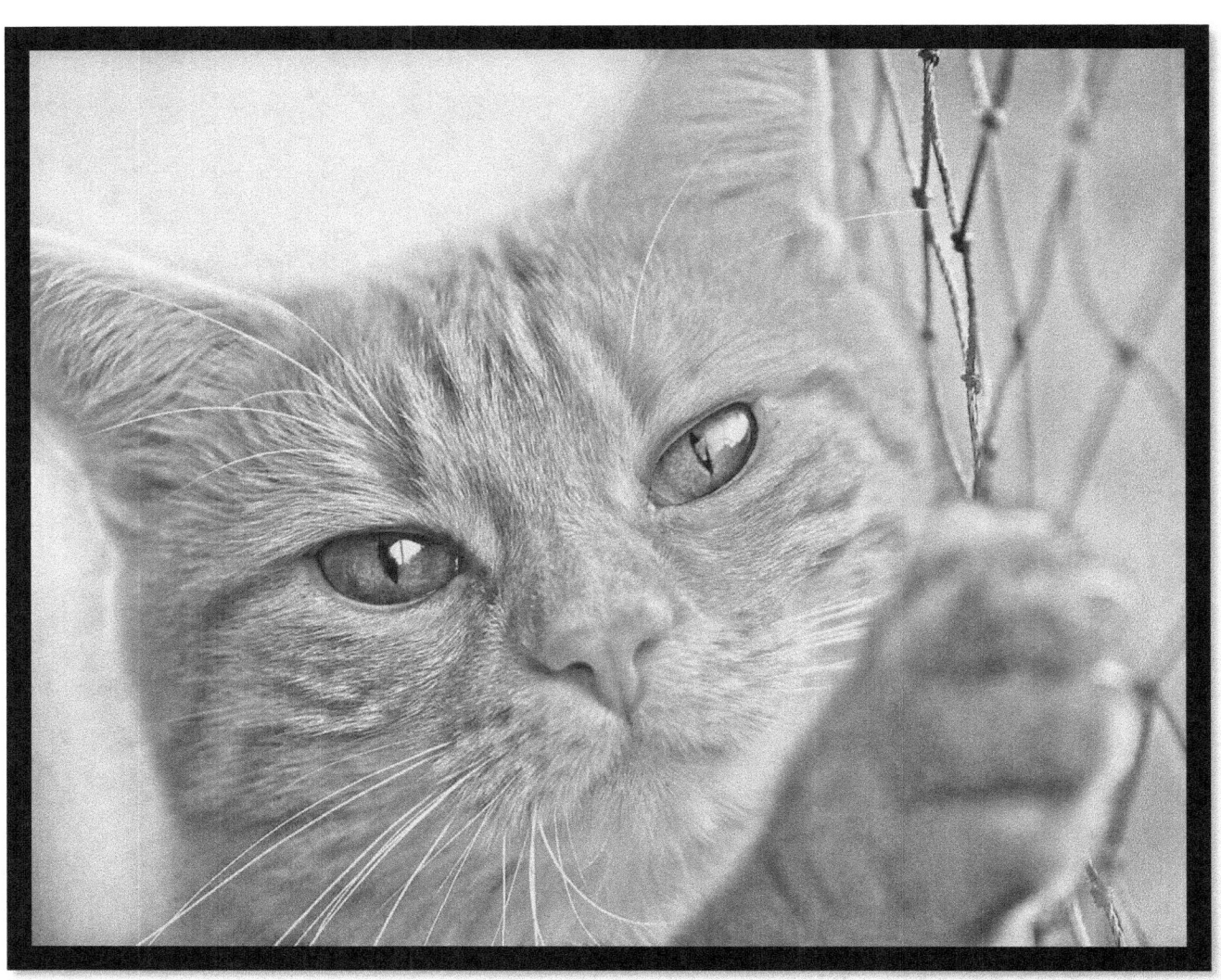

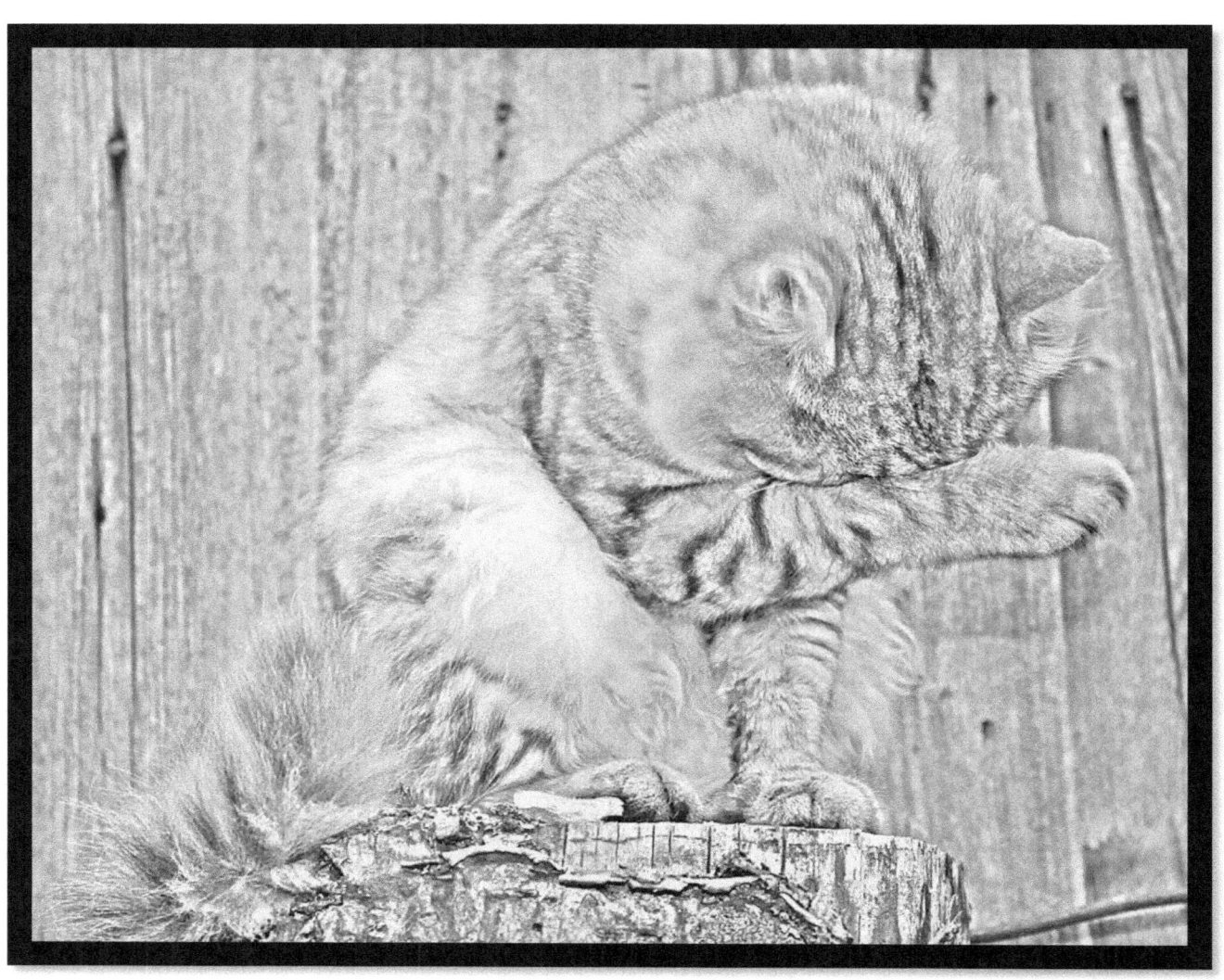

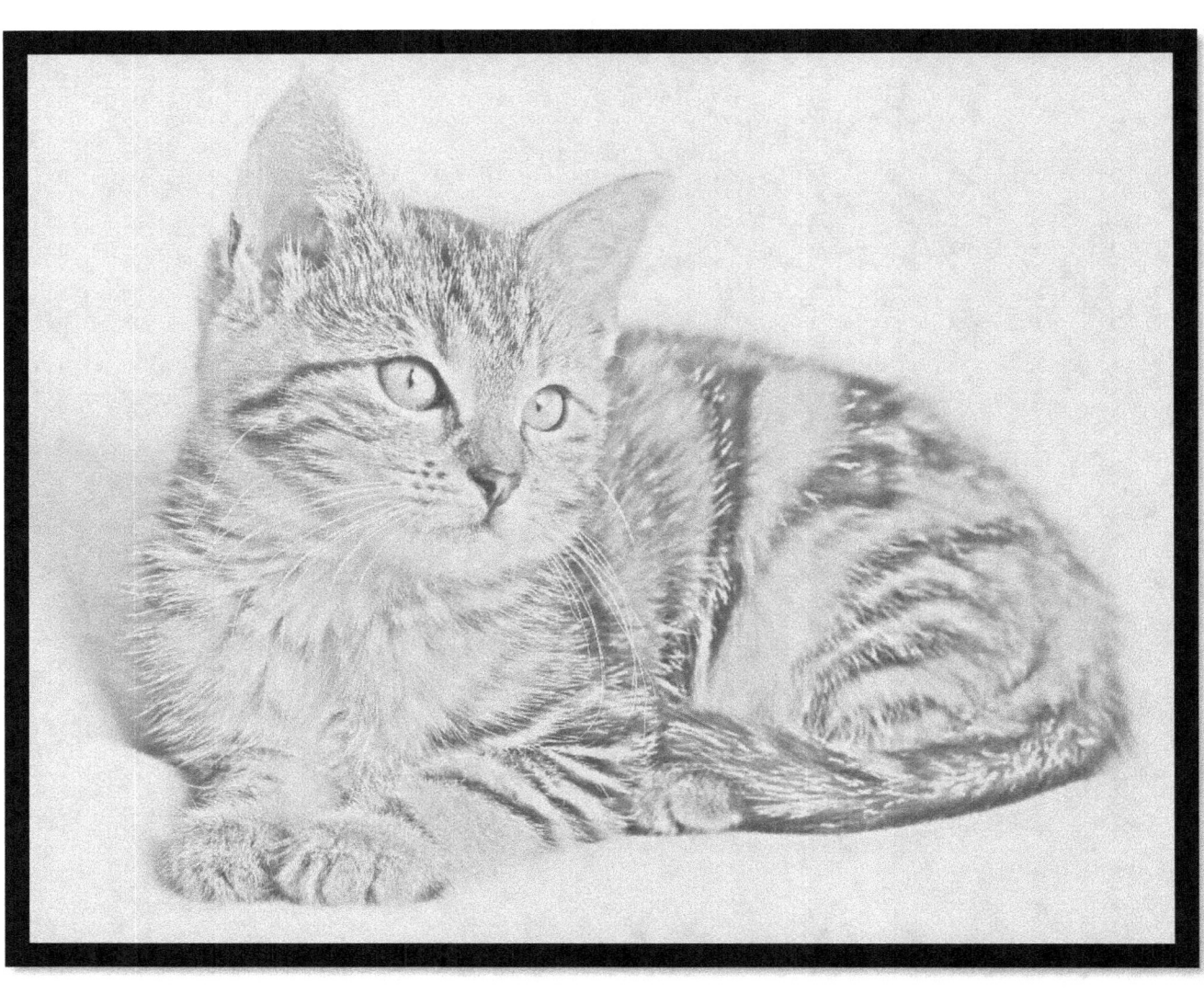

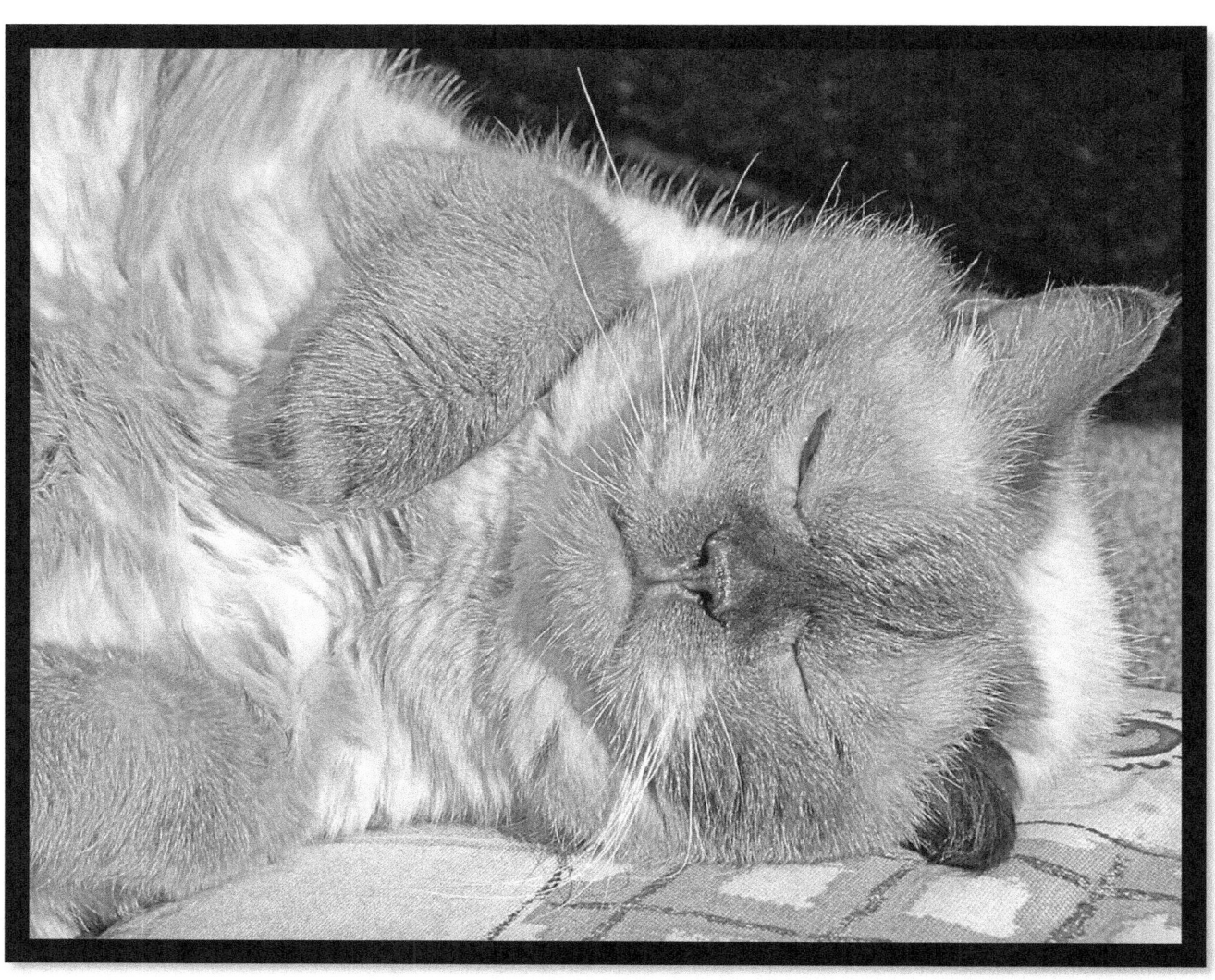

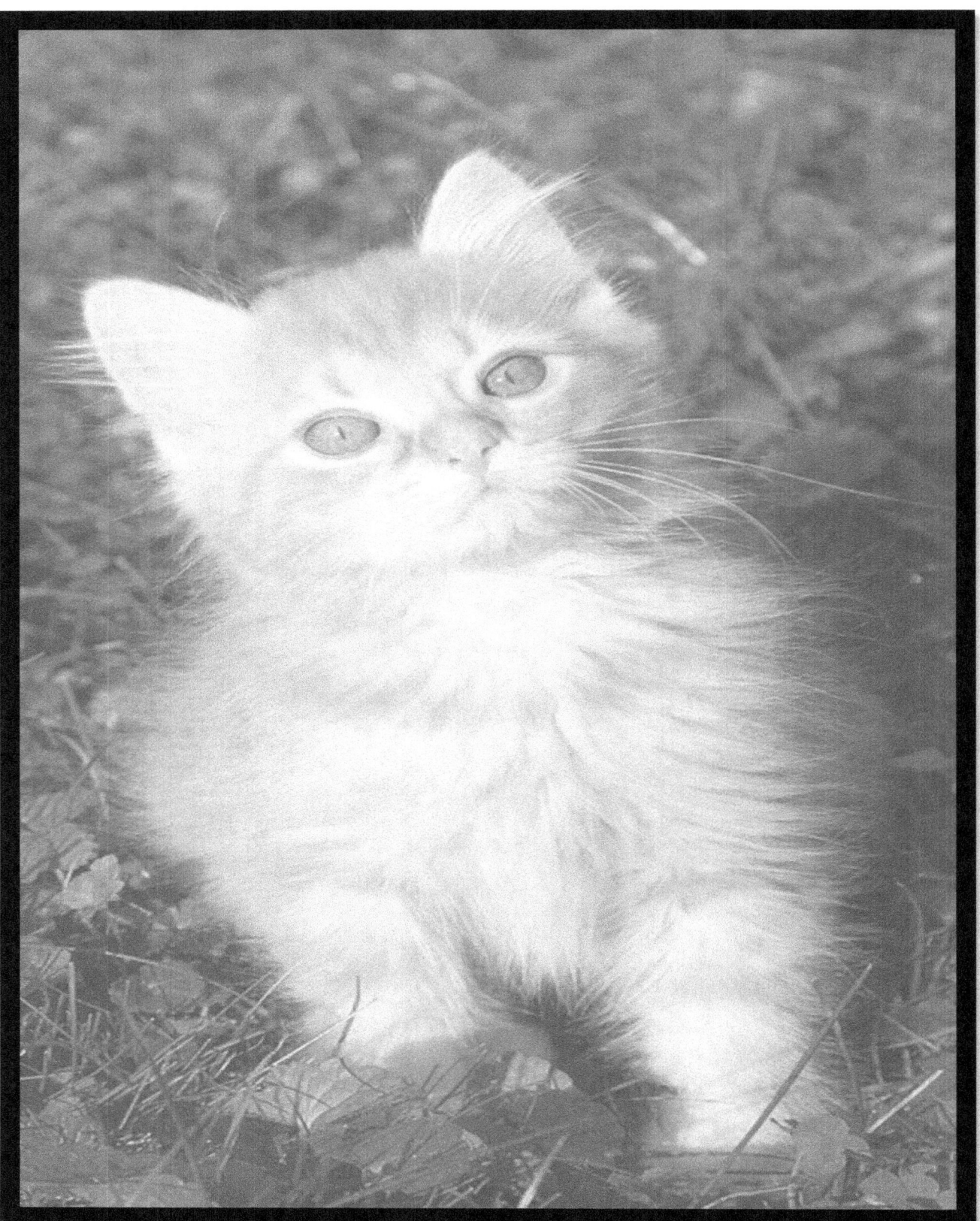

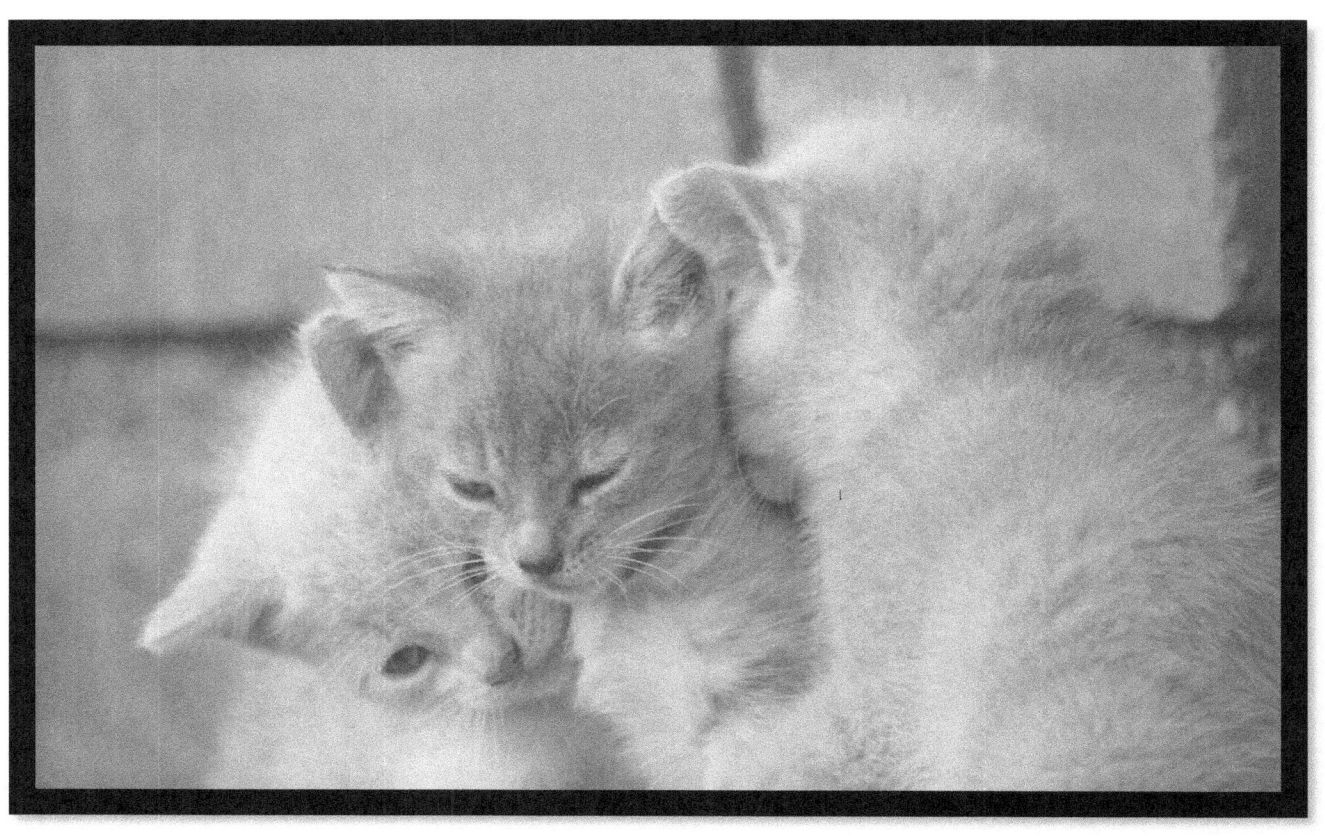

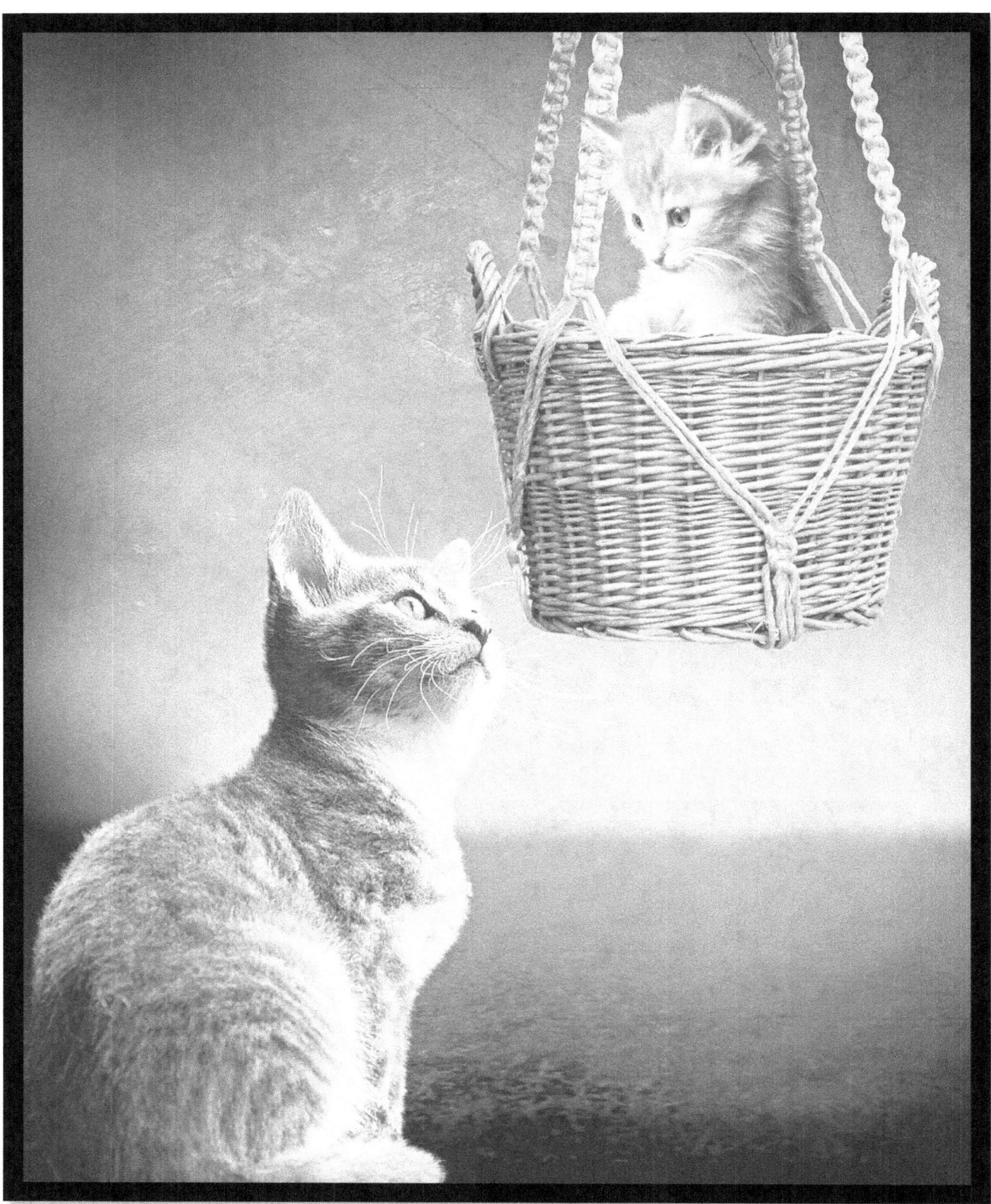

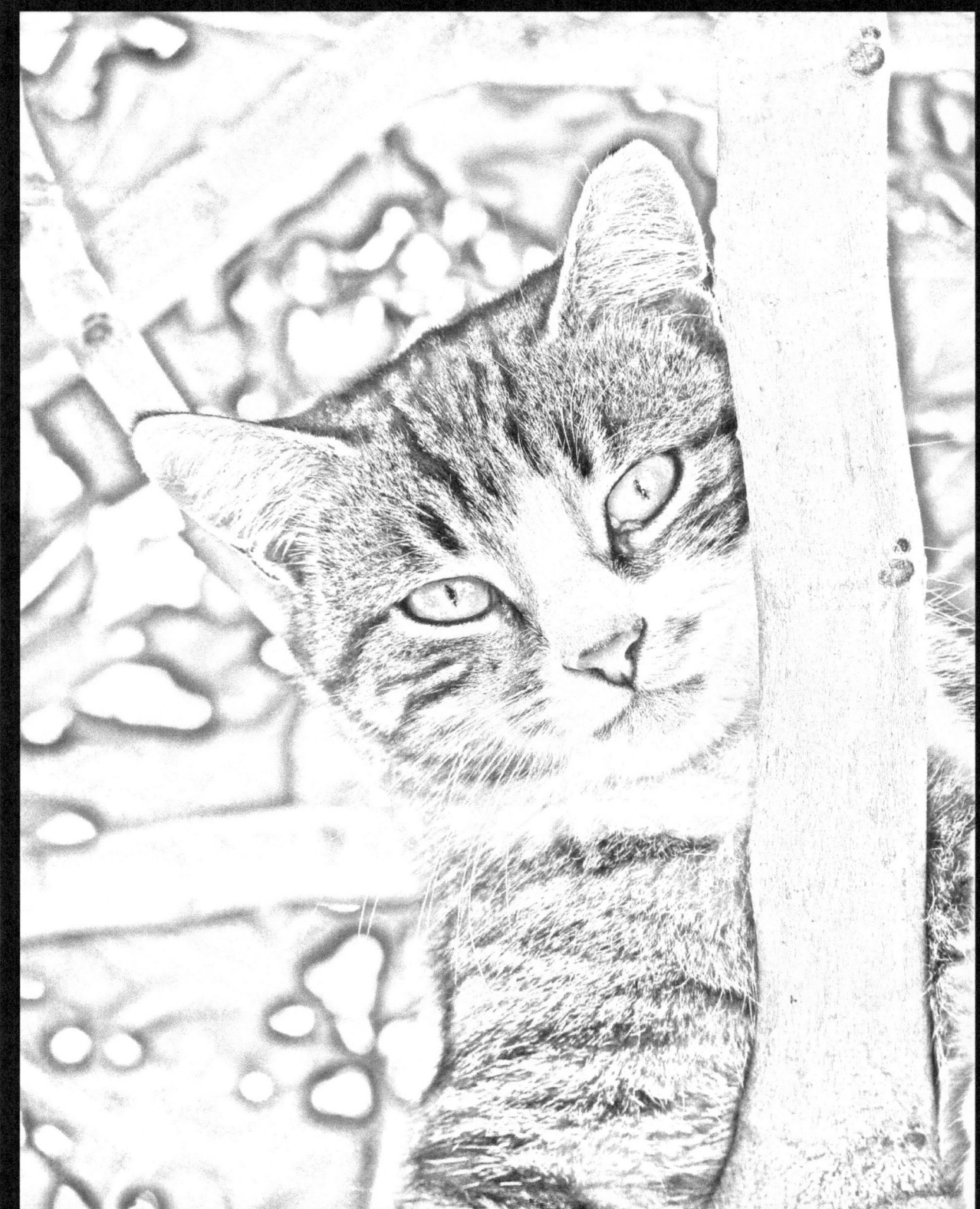

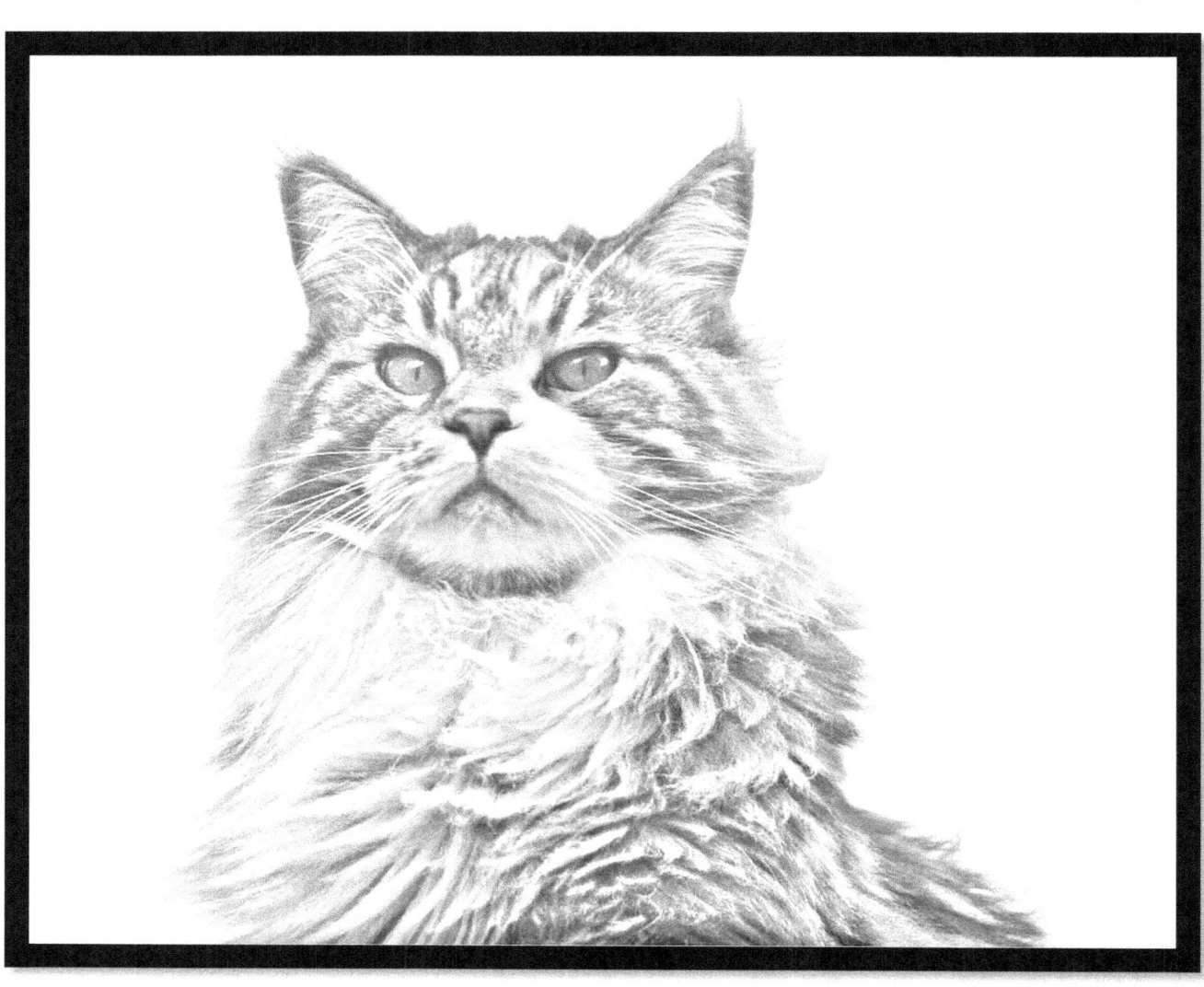

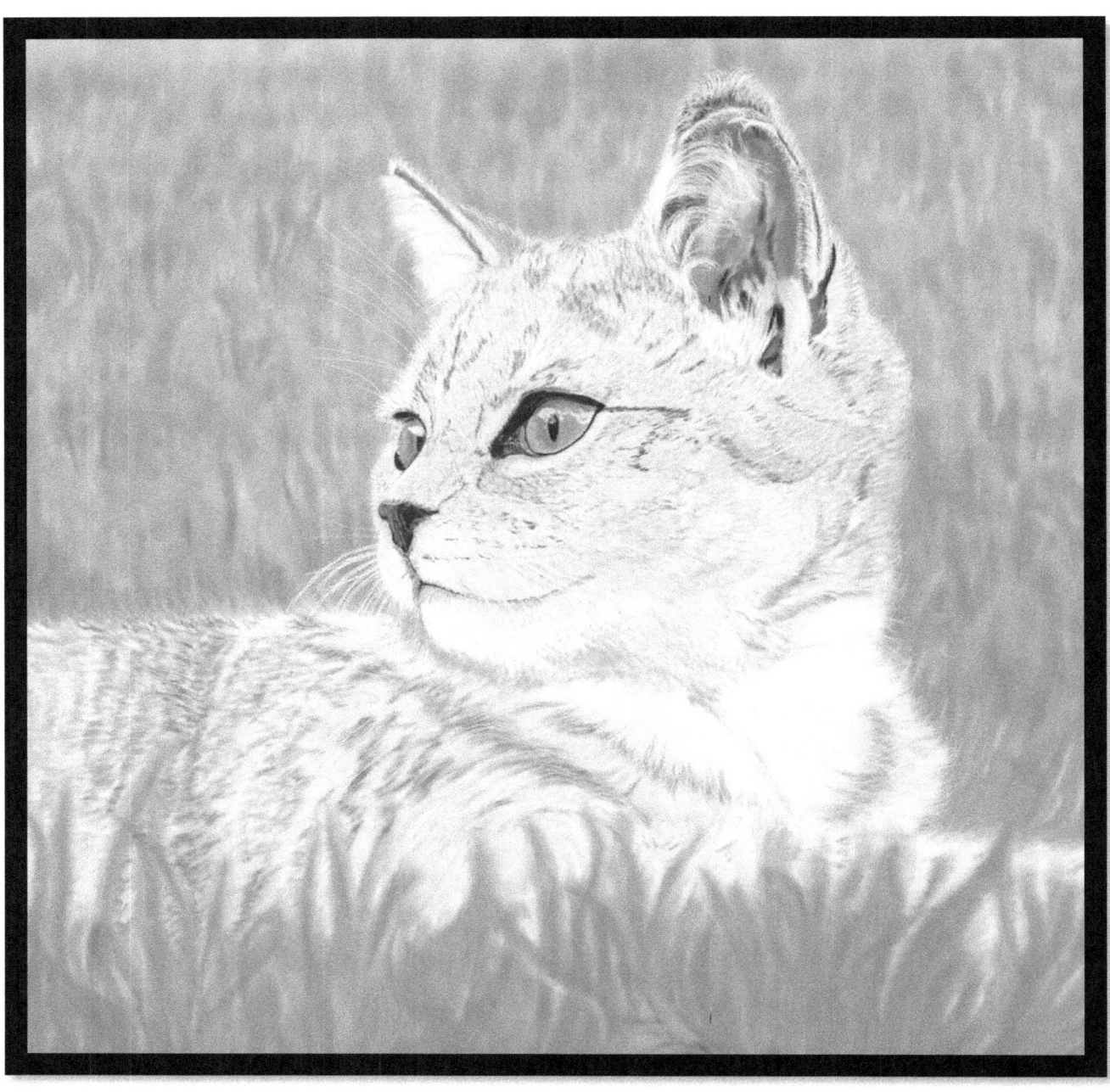

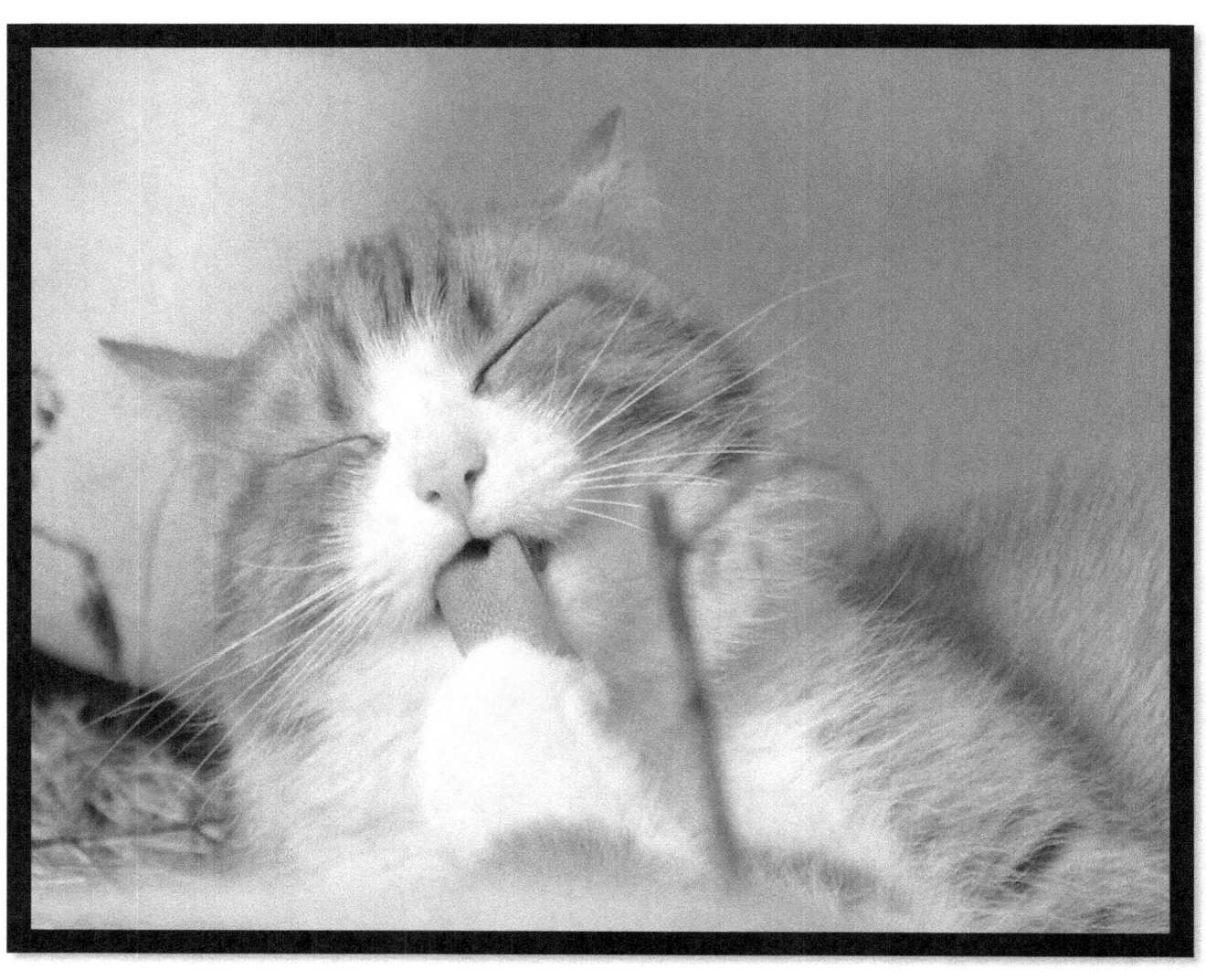

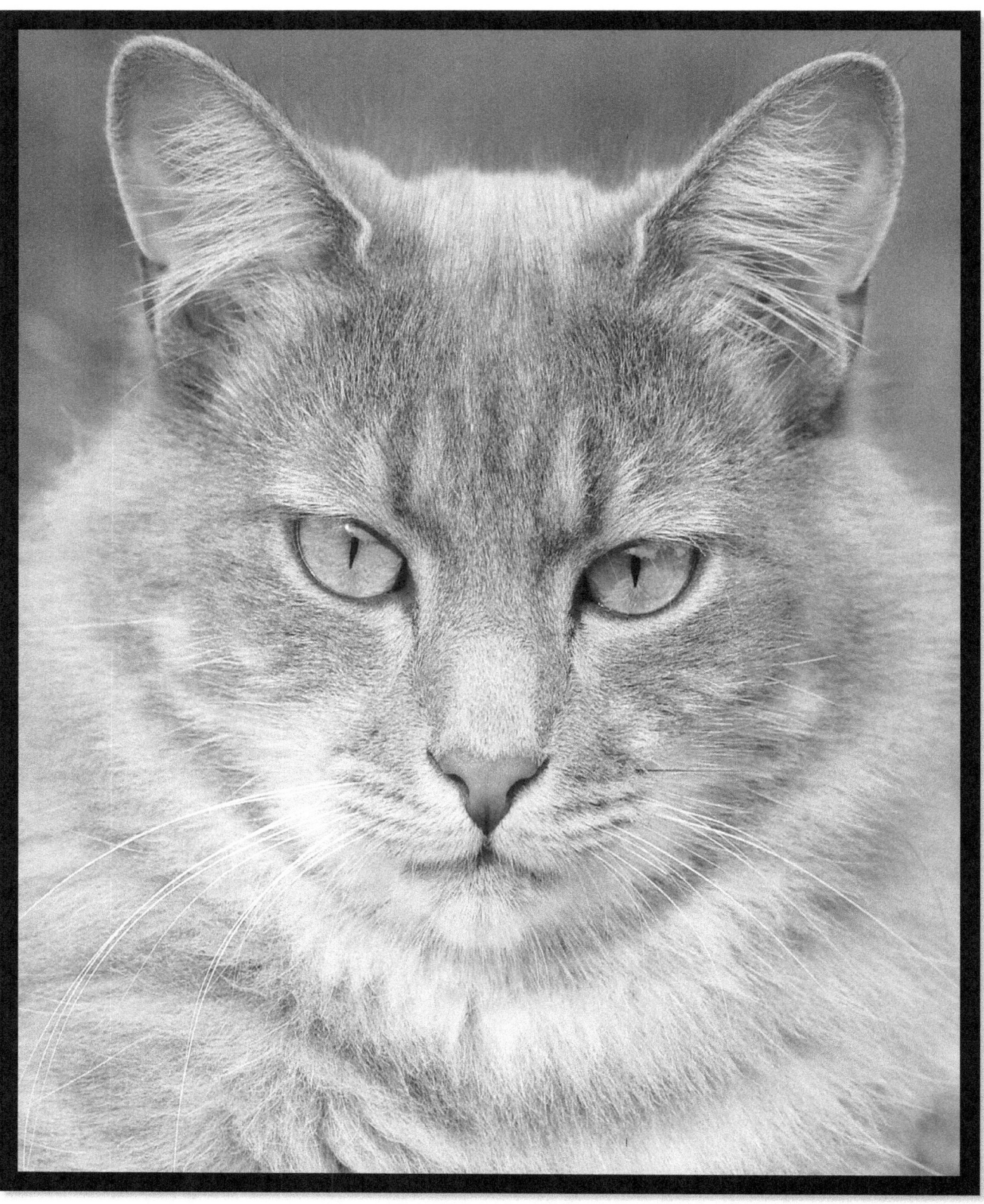

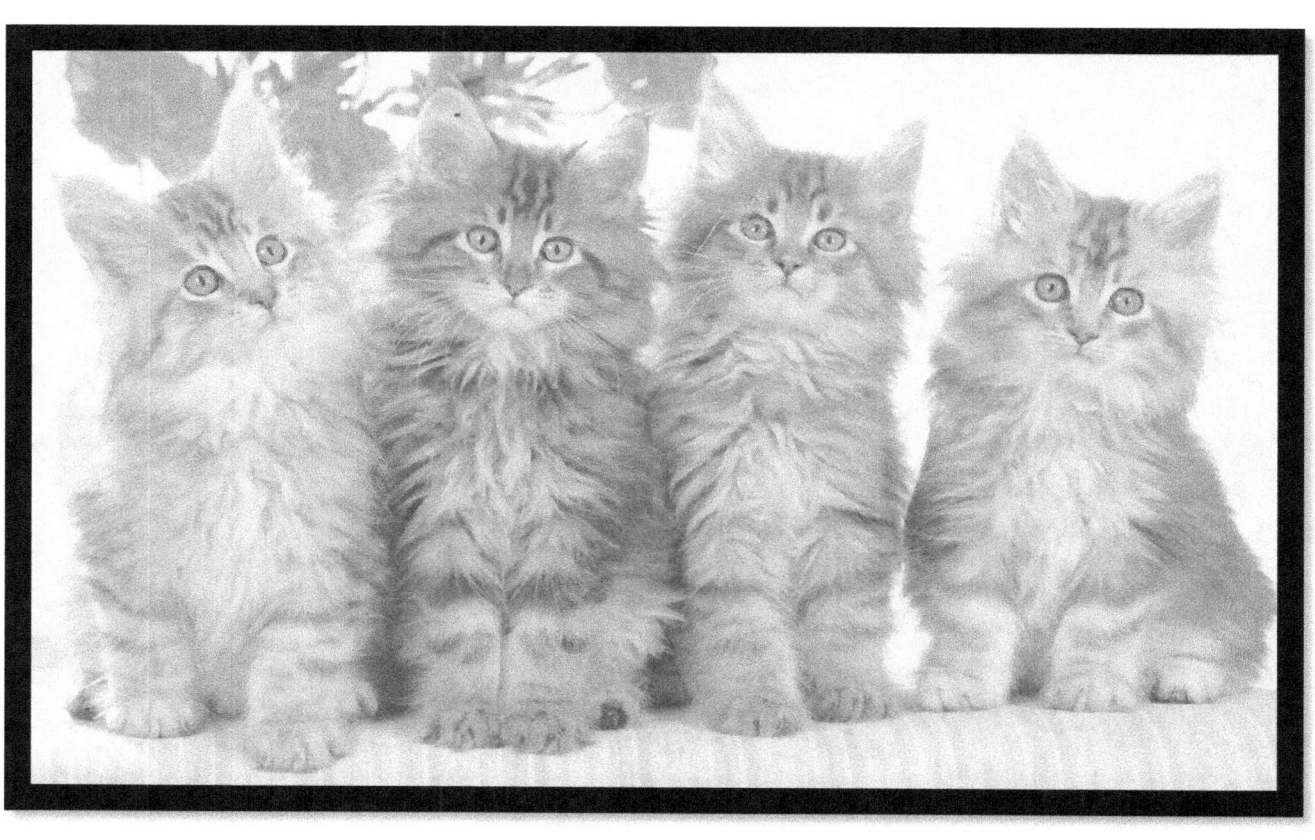

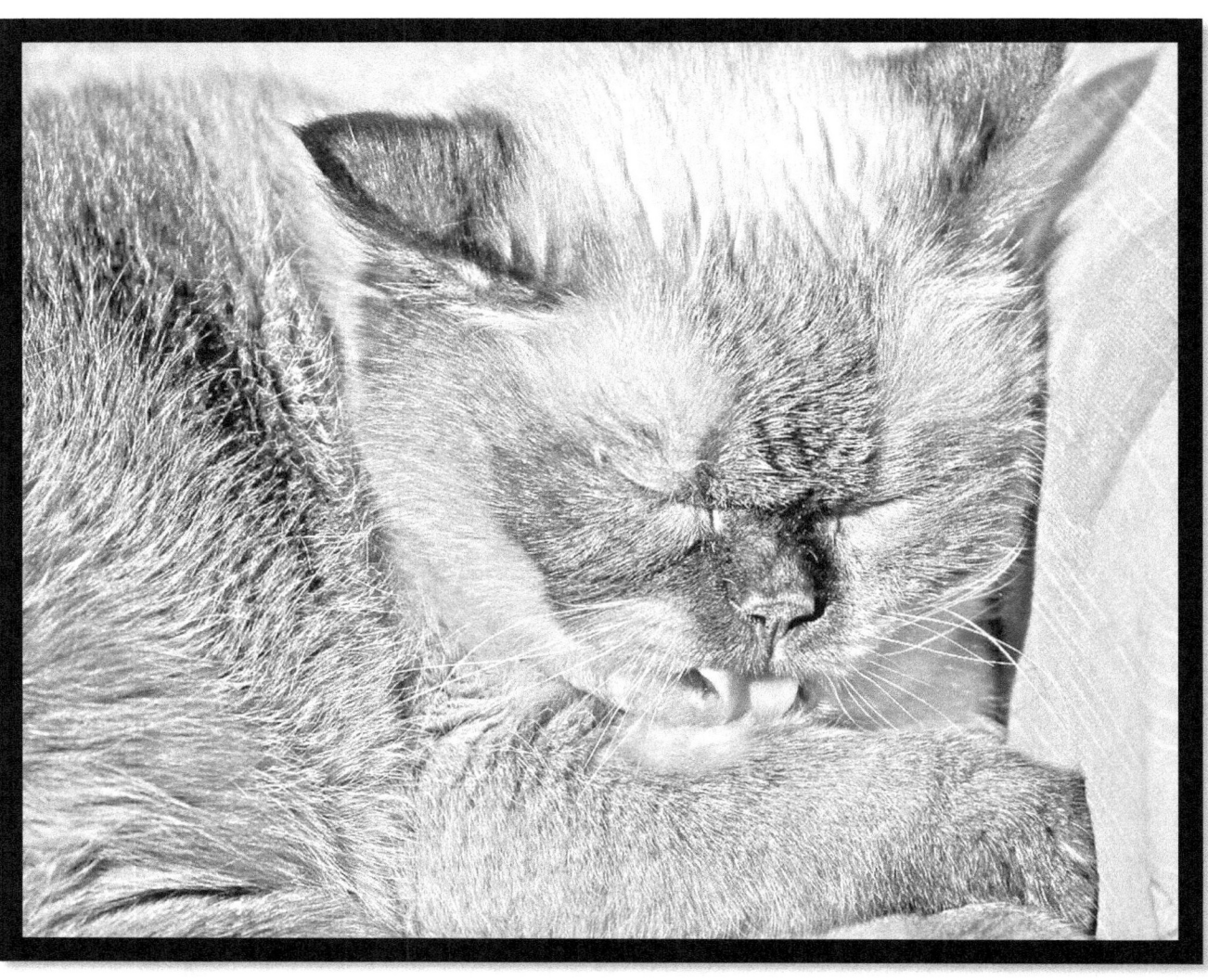

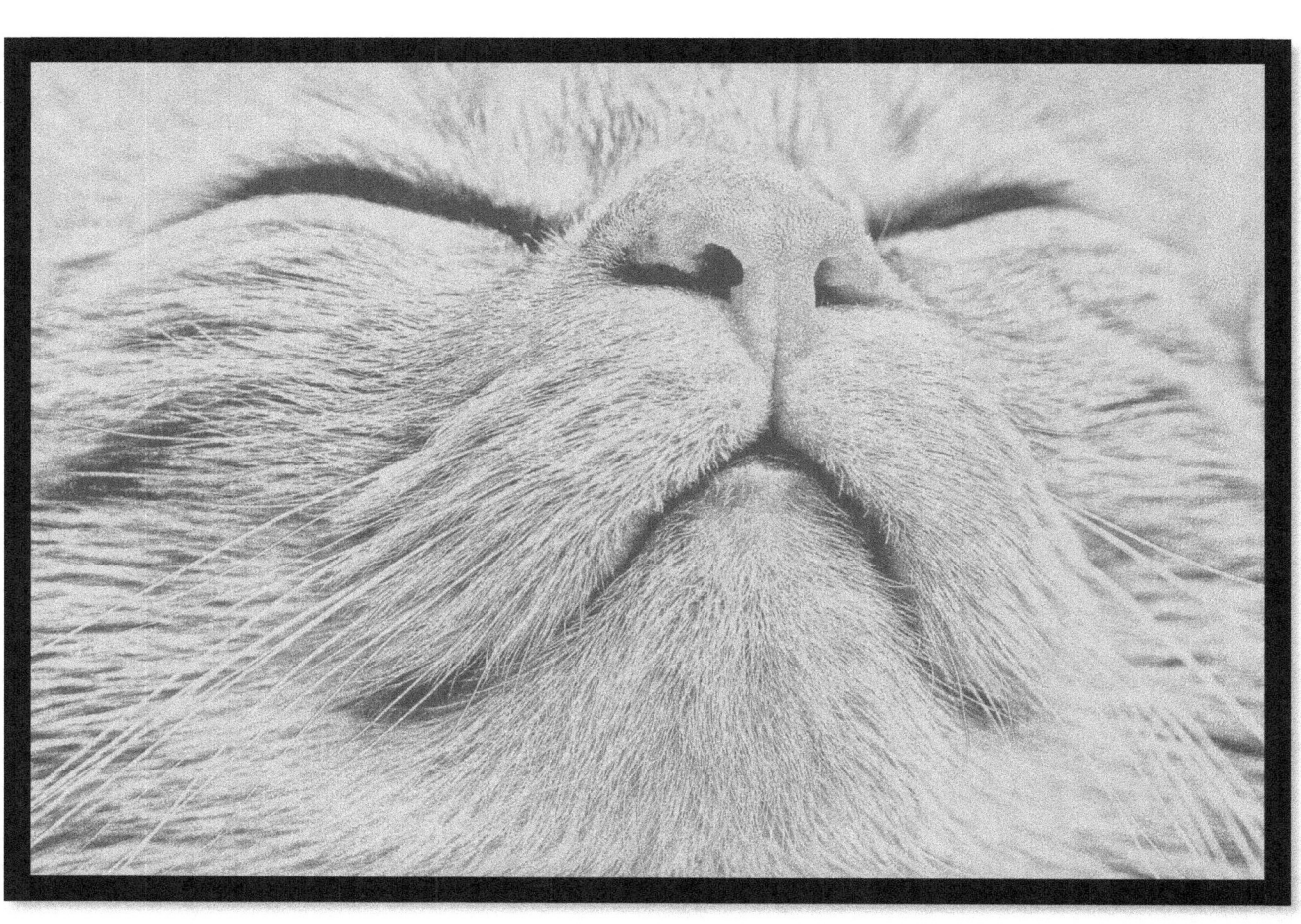

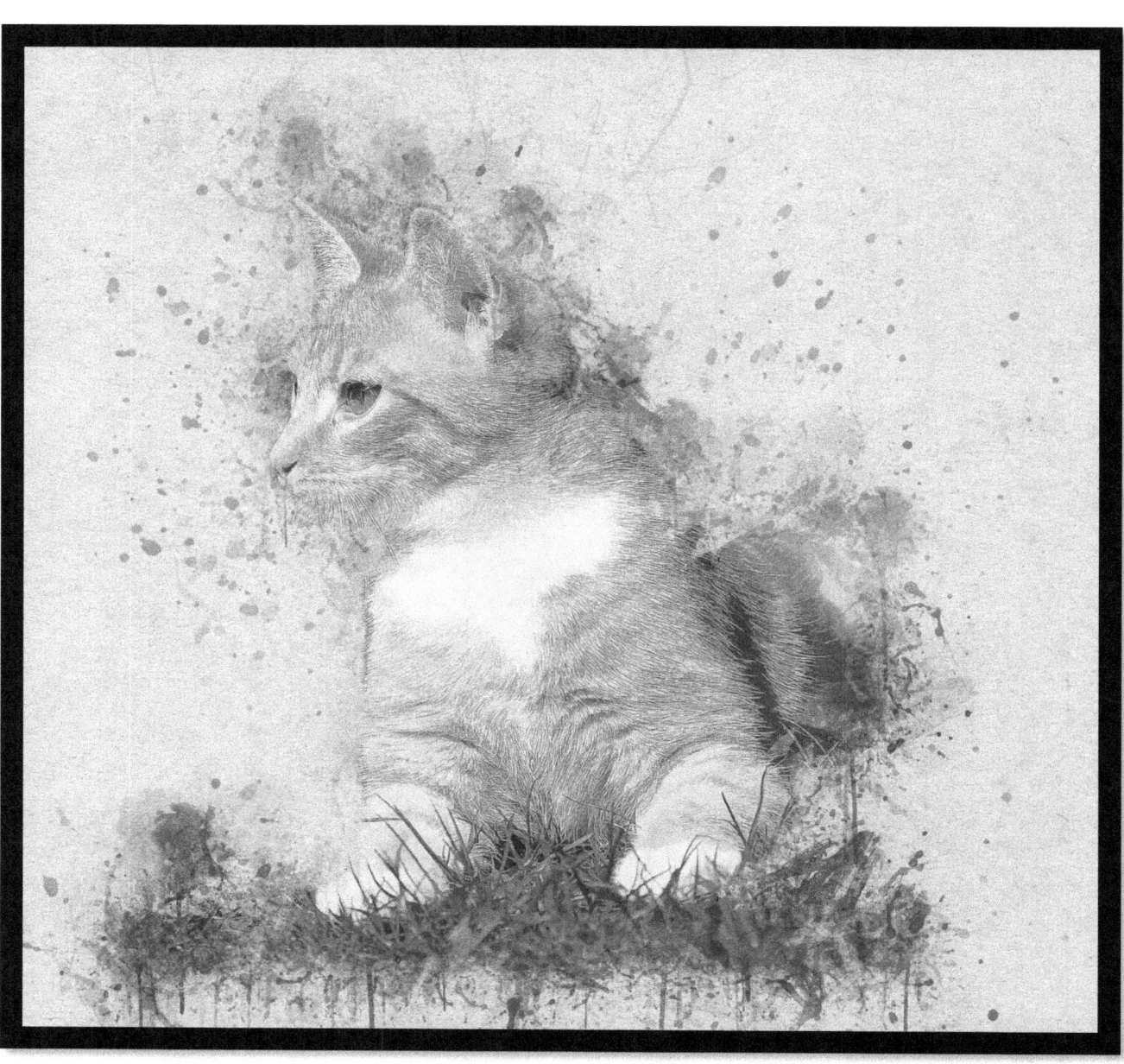

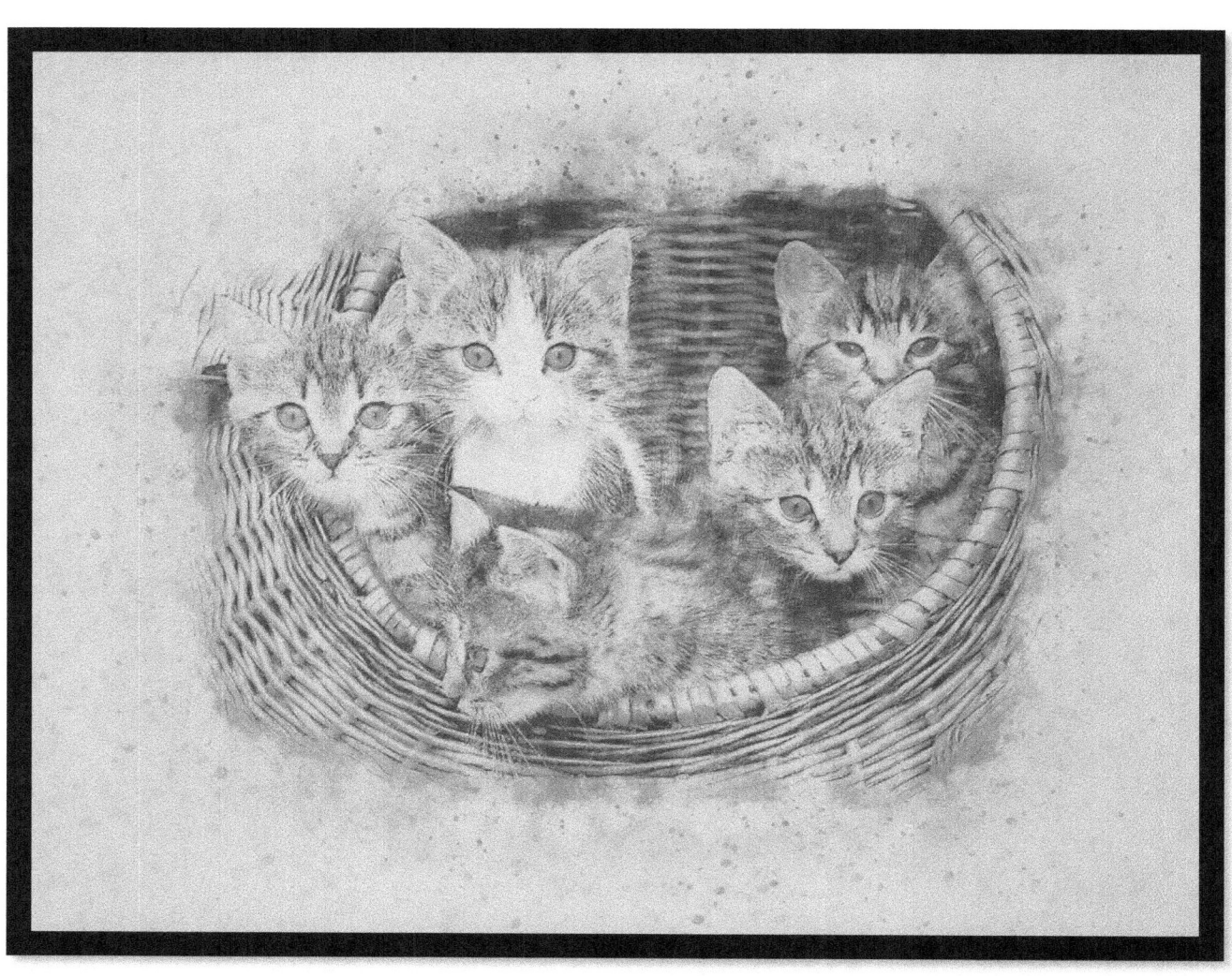

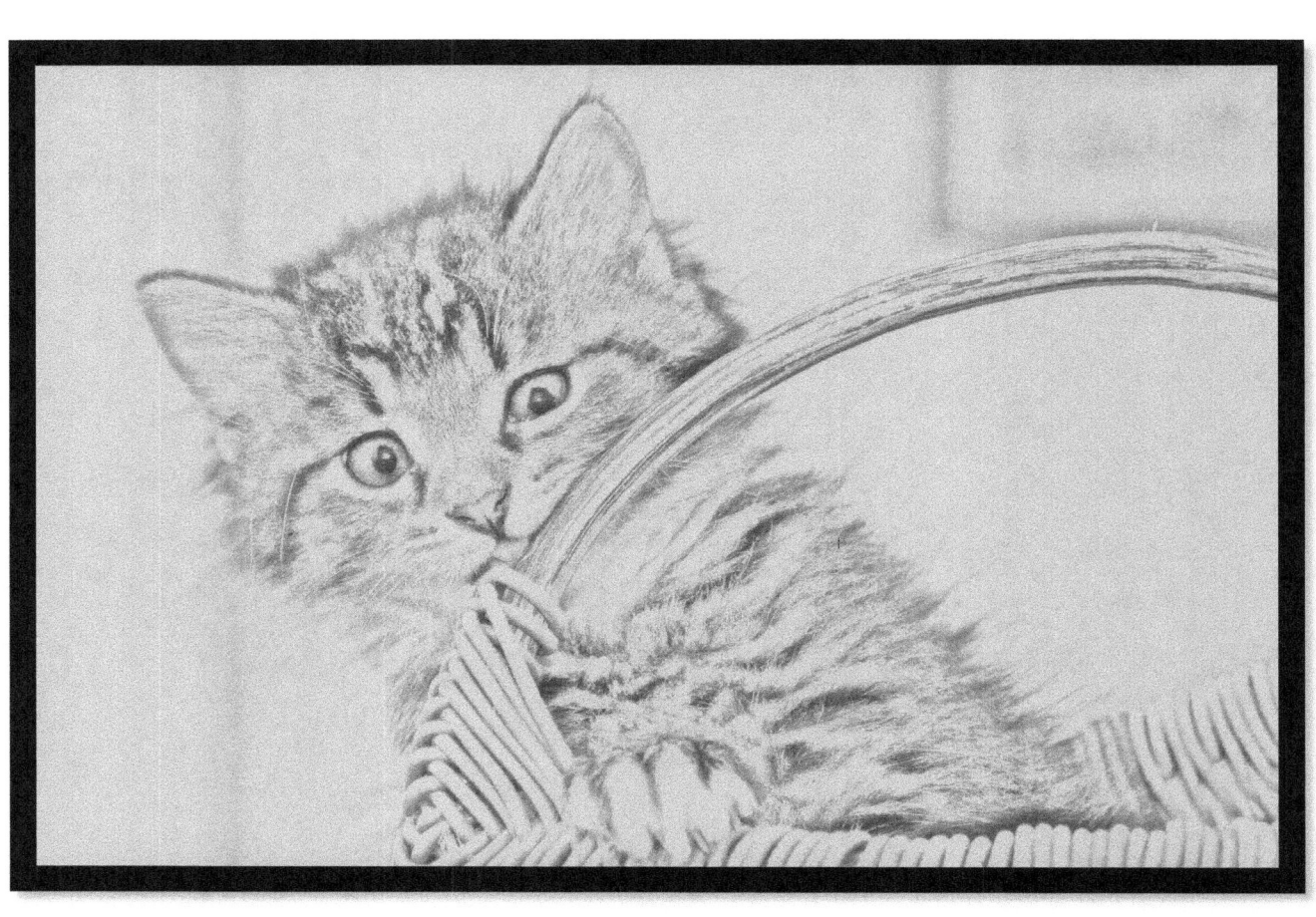

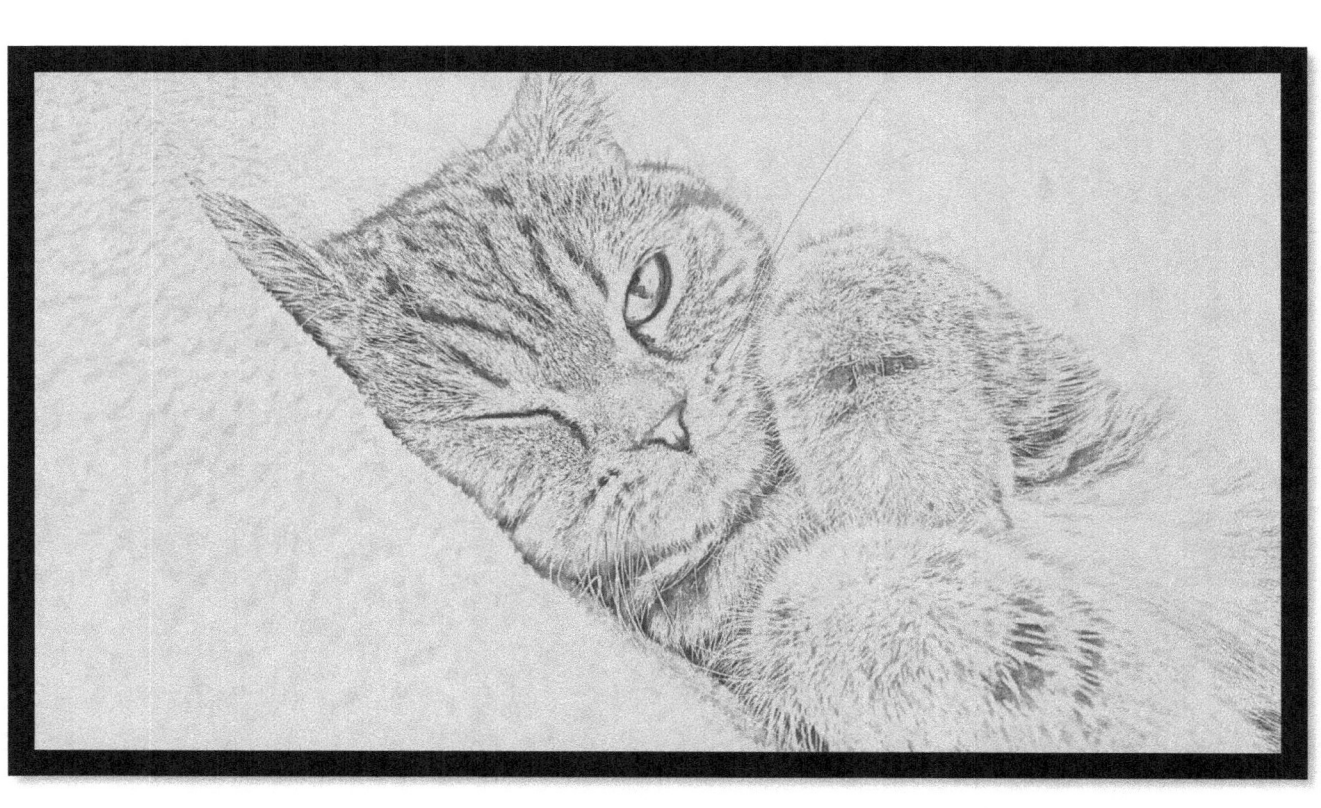

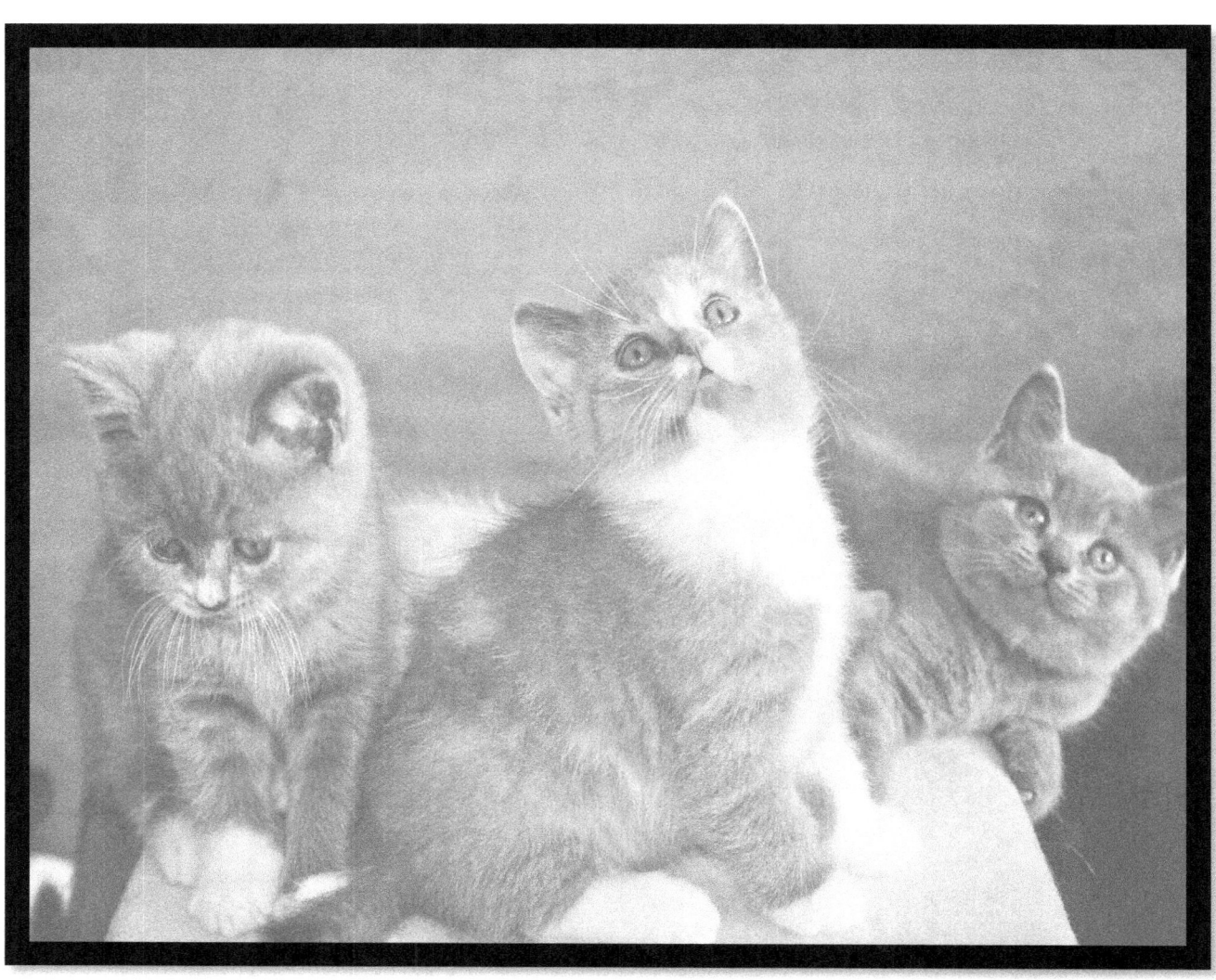

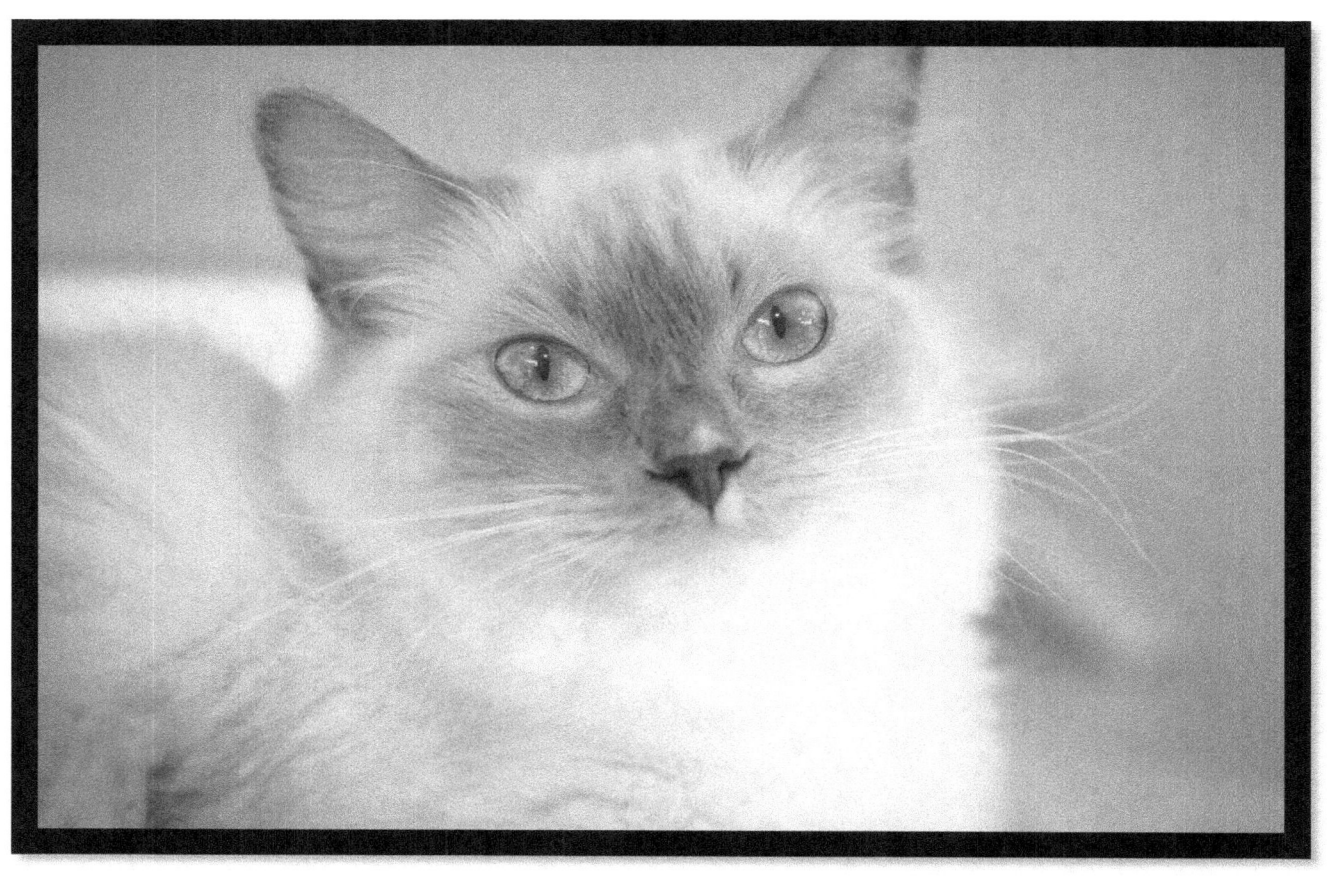

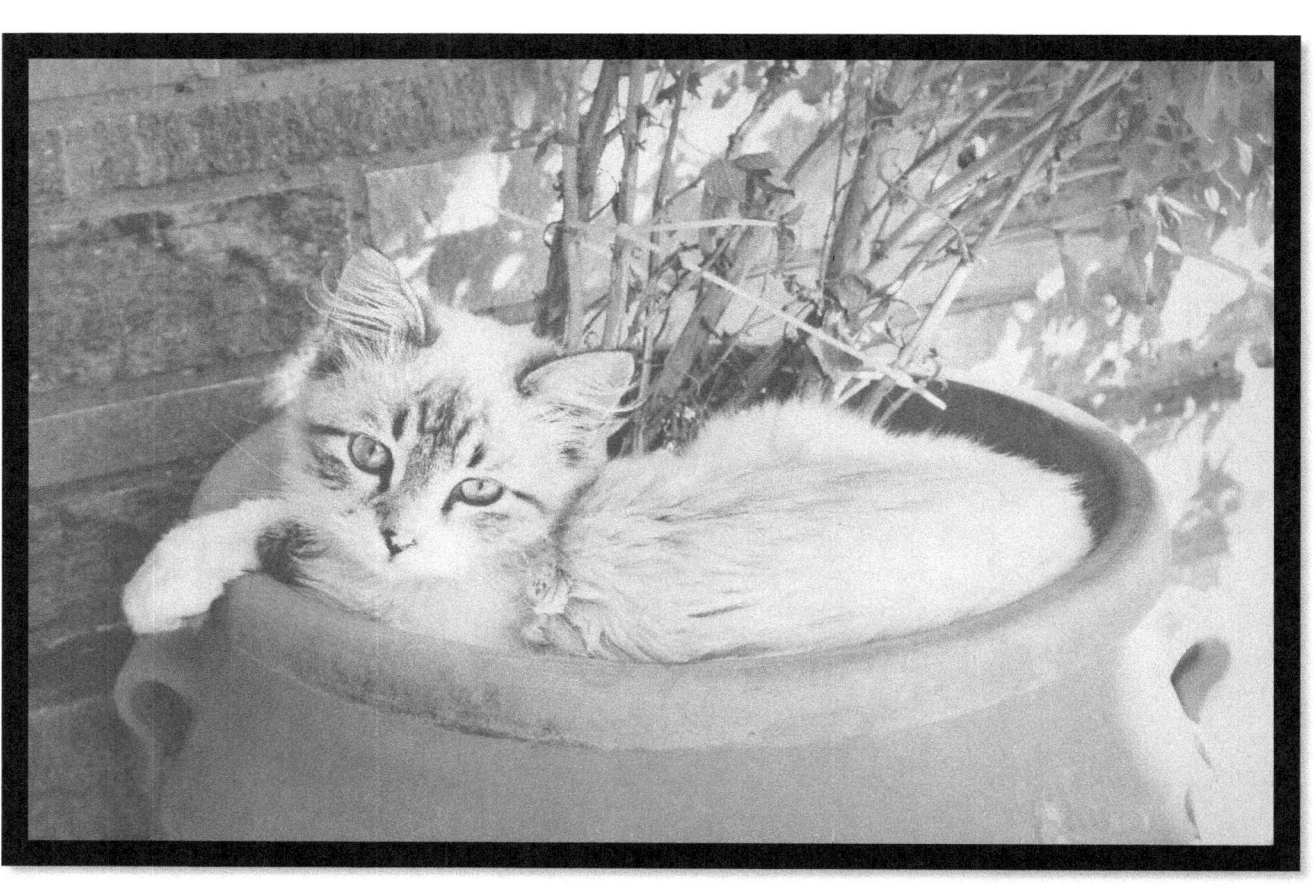

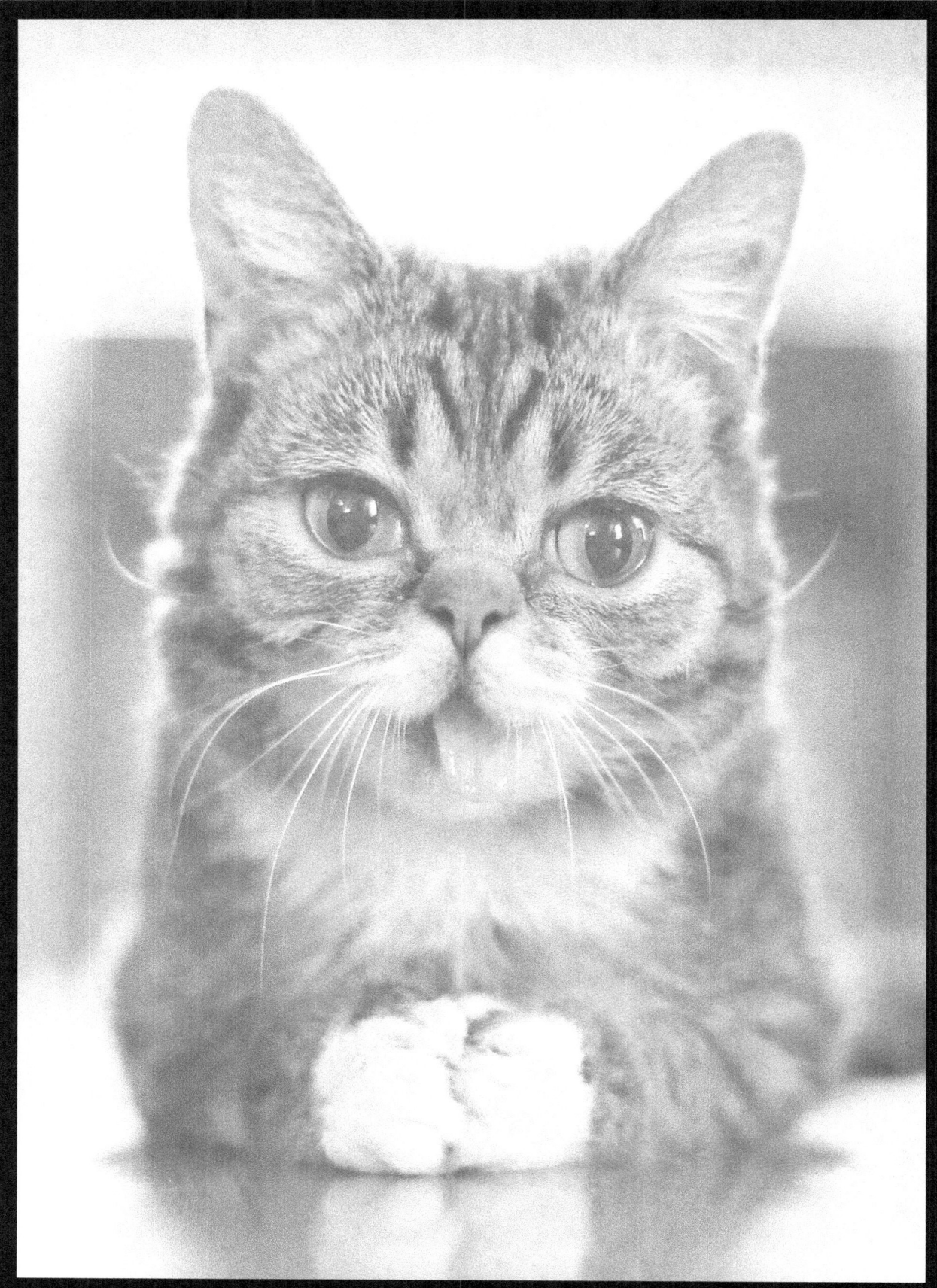

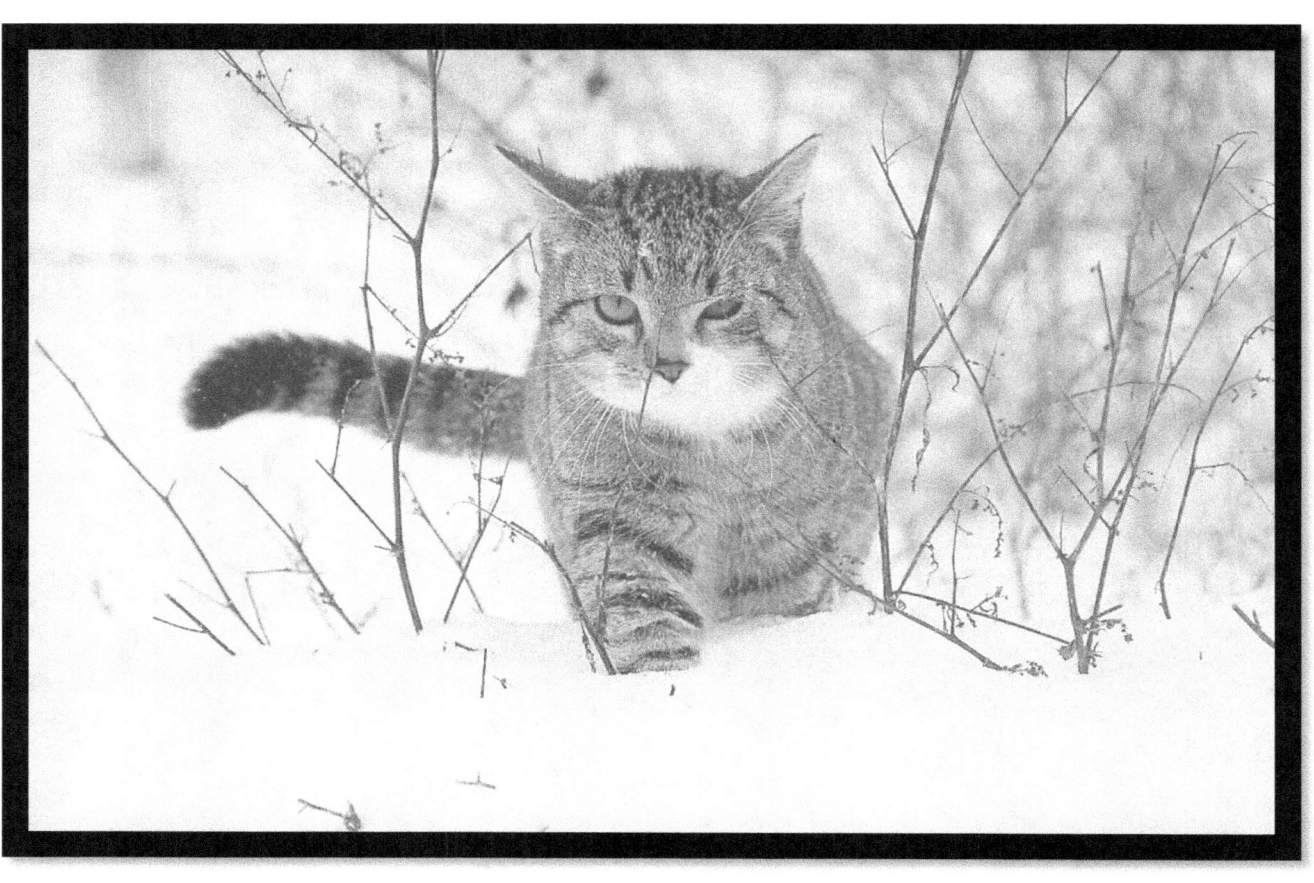

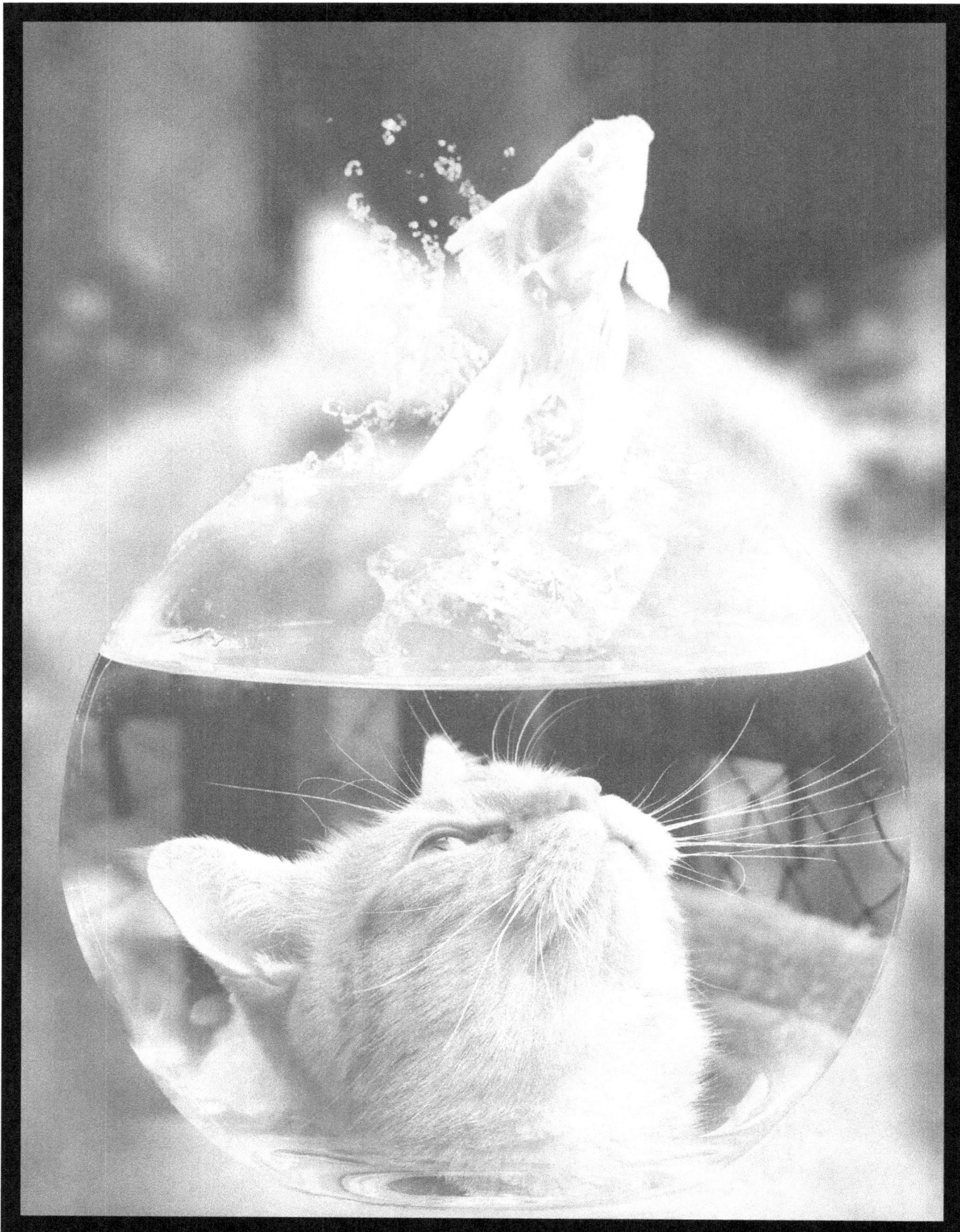

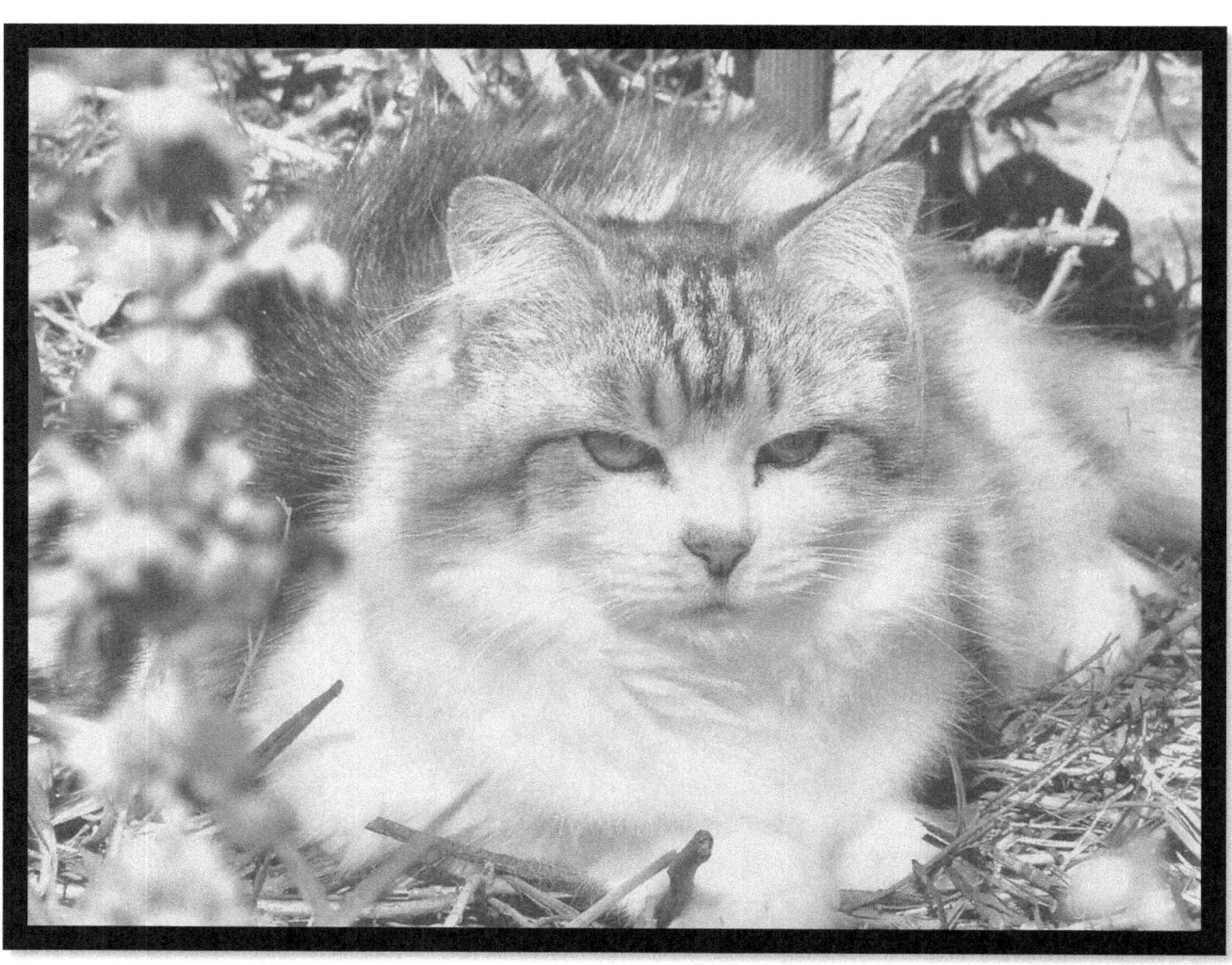

Keep in Touch

For more coloring books visit:

Ordercoloringbook.com

For free coloring pages and tips on how to coloring over gray scale photos visit:

Adultscoloringbook.net

Note:

If you liked this book please write your review.

Hope you enjoyed the book!

Engy Khalil

Other Coloring Books for Adults by Engy Khalil:

Horses Lovers Book: 53 Gray scale coloring pages + free bonuses.

Dog Lovers Book: 50 Gray Scale colorings pages + free bonuses.

Adult Coloring Book Collection Book: 50 Zen tangle and illustration coloring pages + free bonuses.

All the Books are Available at:

Amazon websites & Ordercoloringbook.com

"Use coupon code **"CUTECATS-15%"** at checkout for **15% OFF!** The coupon code is for Ordercoloringbook.com online store only.

Test Your Colors Here

Test Your Colors Here

Test Your Colors Here

www.ingramcontent.com/pod-product-compliance
Lightning Source LLC
Chambersburg PA
CBHW081627220526
45468CB00009B/2336